HEIR

to the Crown

A Mind-Body Devotional
for the Daughters of God

ALISA KEETON

I dedicate this book to my daughter,
Sophia the Brave.

Because of you, my sword is sharper
and crown shines brighter.

IDENTITY

Identity. You might be chuckling a bit, thinking, "How does knowing who I am move me toward my health goals?" You might be thinking you don't have time to dive into this, and yet here you are, still reading! Maybe you've tried it all but know deep down that there has to be more than keeping watch over a number on the scale. I, Alisa Keeton, can say with confidence that knowing who you are has everything to do with how to live *well*. More than knowing what to eat, at what intensity to move, or how heavy your dumbbells need to be, knowing *who you are* is top priority when exploring how to live your best life.

Knowing who you are is a strong foundation for a well-lived life.

Foundation: | foun'dāSH(ə)n | - the basis or groundwork for anything

A deep knowing of who you are at the core of your being is your ticket to ride The Ride of YOUR Life—a life lived "fit" in body (your ability to do whatever dream or desire comes to mind), "fit" in soul (your ability to dream and desire) and "fit" in spirit (your ability to know God, the One who gives good dreams and makes good ideas).

You are made to live a full and overflowing life.

"May God himself, the God who makes everything holy and whole, make you holy and whole, put you together—spirit, soul, and body—and keep you fit for the coming of our Master, Jesus Christ. The One who called you is completely dependable. If he said it, he'll do it!" – 1 Thessalonians 5:23-24, MSG

Can you get on board with the fact that you are not some sort of cosmic accident? That you are not slime meeting time, but a God-idea, highly wanted and created by the heart of a living and loving God? If you can get on board with this good news, you are WELL on your way to getting back what was stolen from you a long time ago in a garden: your identity.

"So God created mankind in his own image, in the image of God he created them; male and female he created them." – Genesis 1:27, NIV

The Oxford definition for identity is this: "The fact of being who or what a person or thing is." You are a very real person reading this page, and over the next 30 days we will go on a treasure hunt to find the REAL you—not who your mom, dad, spouse, child, very best friend or a media-saturated world has *told you to be*, but who the Maker of heaven and earth says you are.

It will be from this deep knowledge of *who you are and who you were created to be* that you can begin to build your extraordinary, healthy, whole and free life.

"For as he thinks within himself, so he is." – Proverbs 23:7, NASB

If you think you are nothing special, you will live a *nothing special* life. It costs us nothing to live and think like that, and the enemy of all that is good and valuable will do all that he can to convince you of this lie.

If you believe you were created on purpose, for a noble purpose, you will rise to live as nobility here on earth. BE ADVISED: this way of living will cost you everything! It will *cost you everything* that is threatening your identity and trying to convince you to live like a cog in a wheel of nothingness, turning on materialism and vain conceit.

MY HONEST ULTERIOR MOTIVE

I'll be honest with you. I have an ulterior motive for writing this devotional. As a fitness professional for over 25 years, and as a woman who enjoys fitness and loves God, nothing gives me greater purpose than partnering with Him in bringing freedom to those who have been oppressed. But something REALLY supercharges me these days, and that's my teenage daughter, Sophia. I am watching my daughter enter the most formative years of her womanhood in a world that pressures her to exchange all that is gold for paper. I see the world coercing the daughters of God to buy into fickle trends and false-imagery. These lies often create disposable friendships in order to avoid the fear of being alone, rather than seeking and waiting for the "iron sharpening iron" friendships to come. Our daughters are tempted to trade in all they have just to survive a surface-obsessed world, a world filled with desires that have no power to satisfy.

As a mom who loves passionately, desiring to be faithful in raising a young girl in an Instagram and YouTube world, I declare that it's time for love, kindness, and the beauty of TRUTH to be proclaimed on the PA system of the world. You can consider this our "Now LIVE" time. Let us awaken and proclaim!

I would like to personally challenge you older daughters of God to go through this 30-day devotional with a younger girl who is coming up behind you. If you are a mom with daughters ten years or older, grab a copy of this book for them too and humble yourself to learn along with them. The younger ones are watching us, mamas. We can show them the way by going first! Let's show them what "me too" looks like in light of God's love for us and His truth that sets us free.

WE ARE ROYALTY

We were always intended to live with God and walk with Him in the cool of the day. Wherever God is, His Kingdom is. No one can ever separate King Jesus from His crown. Jesus's crown of thorns worn on a cross won back for us our crowns of gold. We are God's children, a royal people for His own possession.

"But you are God's chosen treasure—priests who are kings, a spiritual 'nation' set apart as God's devoted ones. He called you out of darkness to experience his marvelous light, and now he claims you as His very own. He did this so that you would broadcast his glorious wonders *throughout the world.*" –1 Peter 2:9, *The Passion Translation*

As The King over all creation, God called us, His royal kids and heirs to the crown, to go into the family business of bringing heaven to earth. Our Father has no greater dream than to see His kids living, reigning and ruling on the earth. He wants us healthy and whole as we extend goodness through the power of God's kindness, wrapped in three of God' favorite gifts to the world: forgiveness, mercy, and grace.

As a mom, I get God's heart. I want nothing less for my children than what Jesus died to give. He came to call us His very own, to be a people of promise, rooted in rest, on mission to destroy the works of hell.

As children of God and royal heirs to the crown, we have forgiveness, mercy, and grace as the weapons of our warfare. These are our weapons for recreating and restoring the world to the way our Father The King always intended for it to be. These are heavy weapons if you have never been trained in how to use them, but once trained, they become light and easy to carry.

THE ROYAL PLAN

For the next 30 days we will journey back to our full inheritance of the crown by following these steps:

BREATHE– This sounds RADICAL, but BEFORE we get busy with renewing our minds, we are going to practice and train the powerful skill and godly discipline of being still and knowing. It seems to me that many have made studying the Word a manipulative way of getting something from God. This heart attitude turns reading God's Word into a religious duty instead of a daughter's delight. You know this is happening to you when you are spending a lot of time studying and talking to God only to find yourself repeating the same belief patterns or actions over and over again. Silence is golden. Silence is powerful! God loves solitude and loves to speak when we are silent and ready to listen.

If you had a friend who always talked and never listened, what kind of friendship would that be? Get comfortable being uncomfortable and get quiet. Ready yourself to listen. I have a feeling this could be the biggest blessing many of you will get out of this quest back to your crown. Hear me when I say that the practice of being still is very important! The ability to be still is being stolen from us in a world that values constant activity. The discipline of being still is a powerful and simple way back to the heart of God who loves to tell us who we are.

If you do nothing else in the next 30 days, commit to 3-5 minutes a day sitting in silence repeating each day's breathing prayer. This is integral to your identity and a strong foundation on which you can build your life.

"In repentance and rest is your salvation, in quietness and trust is your strength." – Isaiah 30:15, NIV

READ – Read each day's devotional based on God's Word. Read the words and let them sink in. Let them renew your mind and restore your true identity.

RECOVER – Take out a pen and answer the identity recovering question(s) provided for you.

RECREATE & RE-CREATE – Have fun recreating and re-creating with God each day. Record what new hopes and dreams you have for each day. Make note of what God is asking you to do to bring life to your body, your soul and your spirit each day. Also take note of what you could do to add to someone else's life that day.

REJOICE – Write a prayer, praising and thanking God for what He has done. Then ask God for what you need based on what you have learned.

Daughters,

Get ready to put your crown on and keep it on!

Let's go!

BREATHE: Set a timer for 3-5 minutes. Find a comfortable chair to sit in, close your eyes, and rest your palms open in your lap or in any comfortable position. Inhale and exhale the following prayer:

INHALE – I am my Father's Daughter
EXHALE – I please my Father's heart

"And a voice from heaven said, 'This is my Son, whom I love; with him I am well pleased.'" – Matthew 3:17, NIV

It is a primal need for a child to be seen by her mother and father. When a forty-week expectant momma crosses the finish line, she inhales one big gulp of breath, grabs the hands of a loved one nearby, buries her chin into her chest and offers up one final life-bearing push. New life comes busting on the scene in a package of pink goo. That fresh bundle of goodness is placed on mother's chest, and then what happens? Two strangers—one who is in charge and one who is totally and utterly dependent—meet. Their lifelong relationship begins not with a handshake but with eyes meeting. In a moment, the thought "*I have waited to see you my whole life*" ties two strangers together from that moment into eternity.

God, your Father in heaven, was the first to see you. He saw your unformed body, looked at it and called it good (Psalm 139). You are God's good idea, wrapped in flesh, sent to love a world that your Father so loves (John 3:16). God, your Father, The King of the Universe, has seen, known and loved you not just when you were born, but from before the foundation of the world. You are your Father's daughter. Being yourself, saying the words that only you can say, singing and dancing in the way that only you can, pleases your Father's heart. He is eternally tied and committed to you.

RECOVER: Answer these questions below by journaling your response.

What do I see when I look at God?

I see god as a angle

What does God see when He looks at me?

He sees my unfomd flessy good body coverd in pink goo

RE-CREATE:

My hope for this day is good sleep

Today I will re-create my **mind** by ?, god

Today I will re-create my **heart** by ?, god

Today I will re-create my **body** by ? sleep

Today I will bless with sleep by god

REJOICE:

Write a personal prayer giving thanks to God for what He has done, is doing or will do. Tell Him how wonderful He is! Then ask Him for what you need.

Thank you god for everthing I need trust.

7

BREATHE: Set a timer for 3-5 minutes. Find a comfortable chair to sit in, close your eyes, and rest your palms open in your lap or in any comfortable position. Inhale and exhale the following prayer:

INHALE – My Father is The King
EXHALE – I am His royal daughter

"For God is the King of all the earth; Sing praises with a skillful psalm. God reigns over the nations, God sits on his holy throne." – Psalm 47:7-8, NASB

It's not likely that we will ever know what it's like to enter the gates of Buckingham Palace. We probably won't ever greet the guard by his first name as he respectfully opens the gold gates and phones up our arrival to a smartly dressed butler who waits to take our coat at the grand entrance. We may wonder what it would be like to breezily pass by the formal front room adorned with opulent furniture and priceless artifacts and make our way back to a splendid kitchen bathed in sunlight with a soft breeze blowing in from the open window. After all, it's in the kitchen that all the real talk of the day happens with other servants of The King. We imagine what it would be like to kick our shoes off and have anything we wish for be provided joyfully by one of The King's servants, to have a refrigerator stocked with tasty and nourishing things that have been prepared for us. Few if any of us know what it is like to be the royal child of an earthly King, to live in a home of privilege, prominence and safety, with a Father who is extravagant with His love and wise when He speaks truth.

Though we may never know what this is like for us on earth, this IS who we are now as royal children, representatives of our God, our Father King. With our "yes" to Jesus, all of us are instantly removed from living as orphans in a shack of lies and become sons and daughters of God who is "the King of all the earth." Just as the prince of England is privy to all the dreams, hopes and plans of his mother, the Queen, so it is for us, the daughters of The King of the earth. He is not simply *a king of a nation* but The King of all nations. Dear daughter, sister-friend, receive your crown and pin it tightly to your head. Never let anyone or anything take it off. When you wear your crown, always remember to sing. Our King's eyes and ears continually roam the earth, looking to respond to the prayers and promises of His sons and daughters. We are people who know who they are and what Kingdom we represent. Take your crown and sing!

RECOVER: Answer these questions below by journaling your response.

Why is it hard for me to see myself as royalty?

Because I have never had royal blood And it is kind dovonin 1millon

How does knowing I am royalty change the way I choose to live?

It dose not I am still the same person.

RE-CREATE:

My hope for this day is nelth

Today I will re-create my **mind** by

Today I will re-create my **heart** by

Today I will re-create my **body** by

Today I will bless Mrs stingley by teaching

REJOICE:

In your journal, write a personal prayer giving thanks to God for what He has done, is doing or will do. Tell Him how wonderful He is! Then ask Him for what you need.

BREATHE: Set a timer for 3-5 minutes. Find a comfortable chair to sit in, close your eyes, and rest your palms open in your lap or in any comfortable position. Inhale and exhale the following prayer:

INHALE – The King is my Father
EXHALE – All that is His is mine

"And if you belong to Christ, then you are Abraham's descendants, heirs according to promise." – Galatians 3:29, NASB

It's easy to think that our bank accounts are running low when we live in a world that requires payment in full to possess what you want. Checking our bank accounts before making a purchase is good practice in a world that runs on currency that must be earned. Asking a first grader how much money they will have left once they spend part of their allowance is good practice, since they will become adults who make contributions and take withdrawals financially.

Believing that you are God's child and living as His child takes you from standing at the bank hoping that your credit will be approved into an awareness that everything you need (but not always everything you want) is already in your possession. Just like a baby girl on earth born to a wealthy father is set to inherit all that her father has earned, so it is for you. You have been born again to a heavenly Father who has created all that you will inherit.

When God called you out of darkness into His marvelous light and promised Himself to you, you were not only given the right to call yourself His child but the right to everything that is His. Endless love, contagious joy, inextinguishable hope – and so much more than money can buy – is all yours to have, forever. Everything that is found in the Kingdom is yours to help meet any need. You are an heir of endless resources in Christ. All that is God's is yours.

RECOVER: Answer these questions below by journaling your response.

How do I define wealth?

_____

_____

_____

What do I have to offer the world that God has given me?

_____

_____

_____

RE-CREATE:

My hope for this day is _____

Today I will re-create my **mind** by _____

Today I will re-create my **heart** by _____

Today I will re-create my **body** by _____

Today I will bless _____ by _____

REJOICE:

In your journal, write a personal prayer giving thanks to God for what He has done, is doing or will do. Tell Him how wonderful He is! Then ask Him for what you need.

_____

_____

_____

_____

_____

_____

_____

_____

_____

_____

_____

BREATHE: Set a timer for 3-5 minutes. Find a comfortable chair to sit in, close your eyes, and rest your palms open in your lap or in any comfortable position. Inhale and exhale the following prayer:

INHALE – I have been crowned
EXHALE – I am never to take it off

"Blessed is the man who remains steadfast under trial, for when he has stood the test he will receive the crown of life, which God has promised to those who love him." – James 1:12

When our King called us each by name to come and live in His home and learn what it means to live a good, noble, and true life, each one of us was fitted for fine clothes, proper shoes, and a royal family signet ring. Lastly, the family crown was placed on our head. No royal child of God is complete without a crown that displays the fact that victory runs in the family bloodline.

Although we now live as God's very own, His chosen and royal children, it is good for us not to forget where we came from. Once living as orphans, thinking and running scared, we were invited to live with The King. He adopted us and made us His very own. The status of our souls went from terminal life to abundant life. Keep in mind, anytime we say yes to our Father's invitation we are saying yes to a battle between our Father's Kingdom and the kingdom of this world. The enemy of our family name, the prince of this world, waits for us to receive a blow to the chin in hopes we will return to believing lies and living like orphans, once separated from our Father's love.

What is our King's directive to us? "My child, always keep your crown on. Always. Every battle you face I have already won! Stand firm and see." Our crowns cannot be taken from us. Only when we hang our heads in defeat will the enemy have a chance at knocking it off our heads. We now belong to generations of royalty and victory!

RECOVER: Answer these questions below by journaling your response.

What victories has my Father, The King, already won for me?

_____

_____

How do I feel about wearing my crown?

_____

_____

RE-CREATE:

My hope for this day is _____

Today I will re-create my **mind** by _____

Today I will re-create my **heart** by _____

Today I will re-create my **body** by _____

Today I will bless _____ by _____

REJOICE:

In your journal, write a personal prayer giving thanks to God for what He has done, is doing or will do. Tell Him how wonderful He is! Then ask Him for what you need.

_____

_____

_____

_____

_____

_____

_____

_____

_____

_____

BREATHE: Set a timer for 3-5 minutes. Find a comfortable chair to sit in, close your eyes, and rest your palms open in your lap or in any comfortable position. Inhale and exhale the following prayer:

INHALE – Father God
EXHALE – I surrender my rights to you

"Yet to all who did receive him, to those who believed in his name, he gave the right to become children of God." – John 1:12

When I was sixteen years old, with sweaty palms and a racing heart, I took a driving test. I passed that test and it gave me the right to give my will some wheels. When I became a certified personal trainer, I took and passed a test that gave me certain rights to work with people and their bodies. A blood test has the power to reveal who has rights to a child and who doesn't. Adopting a child means paper cuts from the mountain of paperwork you and your family will climb. In the world, tests prove personal rights.

The Kingdom of God refuses to operate like a world filled with red tape and forms that must be completed. Belief in Jesus seals your freedom deal. Your adoption papers as a daughter of The King are signed by Jesus with His own blood. You are a child of God. As God's child you have certain unalienable rights – rights that can't be granted to someone else to use or be taken away from you. You have the right to live, even when death tries to deny you that right outside of God's timing. You have the right to the peace that surpasses all worldly wisdom. Your right to be yourself cannot be passed to someone else. Your right to do what only you can do kills the lie of comparison.

The next time the world bullies you into thinking you have to pass a test or follow its protocol to prove anything, be sure to pull out your Kingdom papers. Show the world who you are and who you represent. The King gives you your citizenship in heaven as His daughter, and that means you have rights. Special privileges and an all-access backstage pass to the heart of God became your right when you confessed with your mouth and believed in your heart that Jesus is Lord.

RECOVER: Answer these questions below by journaling your response.

Why do I fight with God or others?

How does knowing my rights as a royal daughter change me?

RE-CREATE:

My hope for this day is

Today I will re-create my **mind** by

Today I will re-create my **heart** by

Today I will re-create my **body** by

Today I will bless _____ by

REJOICE:

Write a personal prayer giving thanks to God for what He has done, is doing or will do. Tell Him how wonderful He is! Then ask Him for what you need.

BREATHE: Set a timer for 3-5 minutes. Find a comfortable chair to sit in, close your eyes, and rest your palms open in your lap or in any comfortable position. Inhale and exhale the following prayer:

INHALE – God is light
EXHALE – With Him I can see in the dark

"For you were once darkness, but now you are light in the Lord. Live as children of light." – Ephesians 5:8, NIV

When is the last time you went for a walk in the dark? Walking in the dark is probably not your regular routine, since the natural rhythm of the day tells our brains and bodies to begin winding down when the sun falls and the dark rolls in. Yet some of the most beautiful things can be seen at night, as darkness provides the perfect backdrop for light to take center stage and steal the show. The stars, the moon, and even the glow of city lights from a mountaintop beckon us to believe that beauty is all around us, just as the Kingdom is always near. Darkness is to creation like black velvet is to a precious stone jeweler who shows off his most prized diamond as it dances in the light.

God's love illuminates our souls to see truth that confronts lies. Whether in the light of the day (when things happen as you hope, and you feel a greater sense of control) or in the darkness of the night (when things don't happen as you hope, and you feel out of control), God's love for us does not change. Just as a light is still light whether it is day or night, God's love has no end. The light that is the truth of His love for us can never be extinguished. Darkness becomes God's backdrop that shows the Light of His faith, hope, and love as they take center stage. Believing in your Father's love for you makes you a daughter of the light who walks in truth, a Kingdom girl who is not afraid of the dark because she bears a sword of light. She sees darkness as an opportunity to shine brighter as she rests more deeply in the certainty that her Father is good, remembering that darkness is but light to Him. A light-bearing daughter has her Father's eyes – eyes that can see in and through the dark to find the truth that illuminates the way back home to a land filled with the Light of The Father's love.

RECOVER: Answer these questions below by journaling your response.

What feels like darkness (an unknown and scary place) in my life?

_____

_____

What things can I see in this darkness?

_____

_____

_____

RE-CREATE:

My hope for this day is _____

Today I will re-create my **mind** by _____

Today I will re-create my **heart** by _____

Today I will re-create my **body** by _____

Today I will bless _____ by _____

REJOICE:

In your journal, write a personal prayer giving thanks to God for what He has done, is doing or will do. Tell Him how wonderful He is! Then ask Him for what you need.

_____

_____

_____

_____

_____

_____

_____

_____

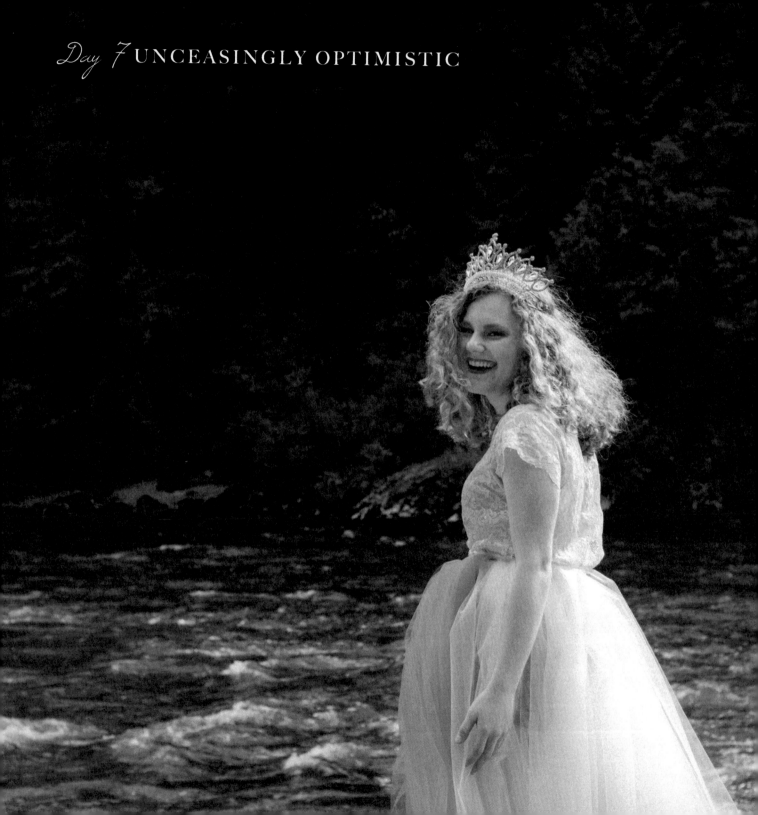

BREATHE: Set a timer for 3-5 minutes. Find a comfortable chair to sit in, close your eyes, and rest your palms open in your lap or in any comfortable position. Inhale and exhale the following prayer:

INHALE – God is good.
EXHALE – Good is God.

"And we know that in all things God works for the good of those who love him, who have been called according to his purpose."
– Romans 8:28, NIV

Let's be real. Life is not easy. You wake up late for one of the most important meetings of your life. Your car breaks down on the way to pick up the kids from school. Unexpected bills show up and wipe your bank account clean just as you were beginning to climb out of a mountain of debt. The world insists on throwing daily "bad news" on our front porches. The enemy of all that is good, loving, creative and kind has no plans on ever taking a vacation. It's the job of Satan, the enemy of God, the prince of this world, to try and convince us that God our King is not good and that He is holding out on us. The snake is still hissing out the same lie that our father Adam and mother Eve believed.

Let us not be deceived. In the beginning there was God, and God was good and still is good. He is the definition of good. All that He created He called "good." God is good and good is God. A daughter of God has set the truth in her heart that her Father, The King, is good. Bearing with something that appears bad with a spirit of patience, kindness, and faithfulness leads a child of God to see that Her Father is up to good in her life and in the world. She will receive a pair of Kingdom goggles to look through that help her see the mark of the Kingdom, God's goodness — rising from smoldering ashes, putting the enemy to shame. A daughter of God knows her Father is good and you can't convince her otherwise. She knows God is with her and He hears her prayers, and that He will not fail to meet her request in the way He knows is best. She knows that if all things in her life are not good then her Good Father God is not finished. Where it is not good; it is not finished. She is unceasingly optimistic.

RECOVER: Answer these questions below by journaling your response.

What encourages my heart about God's goodness?

_____

_____

What do I need to know about God's goodness?

_____

_____

RE-CREATE:

My hope for this day is _____

Today I will re-create my **mind** by _____

Today I will re-create my **heart** by _____

Today I will re-create my **body** by _____

Today I will bless _____ by _____

REJOICE:

In your journal, write a personal prayer giving thanks to God for what He has done, is doing or will do. Tell Him how wonderful He is! Then ask Him for what you need.

_____

_____

_____

_____

_____

_____

_____

_____

BREATHE: Set a timer for 3-5 minutes. Find a comfortable chair to sit in, close your eyes, and rest your palms open in your lap or in any comfortable position. Inhale and exhale the following prayer:

INHALE – God's love in me
EXHALE – God's love on me

"But the Lord said to Samuel, "Do not look on his appearance or on the height of his stature, because I have rejected him. For the Lord sees not as man sees: man looks on the outward appearance, but the Lord looks on the heart." –1 Samuel 16:7

Every year at Christmastime my friends and I exchange gifts, white elephant style. It's a gift giving game where everyone brings a wrapped gift, concealing a unique trinket inside. Depending on how well a gift is wrapped is often an indicator of how quickly the item will move on in the white elephant market. Choosing a gift based on what is seen on the outside in no way insures that a high-quality gift will be yours. In fact, the most fun is seeing how obnoxious of a gift you can give to someone without their knowing. Distracting with pretty paper, bows, and ribbons is a good way to get someone to unknowingly choose a toilet seat cover!

It's a good thing God cannot be fooled. His eyes see past the shape of a body straight to the heart where real life flows from. Nothing God creates is made to fool us or make us foolish. As His creation, we become foolish by believing we can outwit God by projecting a perfect "put together" image to an imperfect world. We fuss and fight, conforming ourselves to look like one another, starving ourselves to be smaller, focusing most on what can be seen. Some daughters take a pass on representing the royal family so that they can present themselves to the kingdom of this world. They hope it will approve and satisfy their desires, but they were meant to desire The King and His Kingdom first and most. We must never put our hope in what is seen but we can always put our hope in God who alone can see our heart. He sees our heart and says, "It is good!"

RECOVER: Answer these questions below by journaling your response.

How am I fooled when I focus on the outside?

_____

_____

What can I do to see past what is seen?

_____

_____

RE-CREATE:

My hope for this day is _____

Today I will re-create my **mind** by _____

Today I will re-create my **heart** by _____

Today I will re-create my **body** by _____

Today I will bless _____ by _____

REJOICE:

In your journal, write a personal prayer giving thanks to God for what He has done, is doing or will do. Tell Him how wonderful He is! Then ask Him for what you need.

_____

_____

_____

_____

_____

_____

_____

_____

_____

BREATHE: Set a timer for 3-5 minutes. Find a comfortable chair to sit in, close your eyes, and rest your palms open in your lap or in any comfortable position. Inhale and exhale the following prayer:

INHALE – God fights for me,
EXHALE – so I can be still

"The Lord will fight for you, you need only to be still."
– Exodus 14:14, NIV

When I picture a royal woman, a woman who is heir to a kingdom, I don't picture the woman frenzied, running late for the ball, the banquet or an important meeting with heads of state. Nor do I remember the fairy tale heroine, Cinderella, the maid-servant turned princess for a day, hike up her gown and hightail it from the prince in fear that her cover is blown because her dream event came with an expiration hour.

Instead, I remember that God, our King, is seated on His throne. He is not fretting or feeling the need to stay on his toes because there may be a surprise attack by surrounding enemies or a change of plans at midnight. Every battle has been won at the cross and His term in office will never end. His dreams and desires for His daughters do not come with an expiration date. No one is too old, too young, too early or too late to collect her inherited promises from her Father, The King. There is no need for a royal daughter to run in fear or hide in shame. She rests in the strength of her King and runs just to feel the wind moving against her face and through her hair.

RECOVER: Answer these questions below by journaling your response.

Do I have a hard time resting? If yes, Why?

_____

_____

What lie(s) do I believe that keeps me from being a woman at rest?

_____

_____

RE-CREATE:

My hope for this day is _____

Today I will re-create my **mind** by _____

Today I will re-create my **heart** by _____

Today I will re-create my **body** by _____

Today I will bless _____ by _____

REJOICE:

In your journal, write a personal prayer giving thanks to God for what He has done, is doing or will do. Tell Him how wonderful He is! Then ask Him for what you need.

_____

_____

_____

_____

_____

_____

_____

_____

_____

_____

BREATHE: Set a timer for 3-5 minutes. Find a comfortable chair to sit in, close your eyes, and rest your palms open in your lap or in any comfortable position. Inhale and exhale the following prayer:

INHALE – My Father in heaven
EXHALE – loves to listen to me

"But if anyone is a worshiper of God and does his will, God listens to him." – John 9:31, NRSV

"Mom. Mom. Mom. Mom. MOOOOMMM!" Any mother of a toddler can tell you that she has been haunted and hunted by those words, probably at the same time someone is clinging to her leg and pulling at her shirt with sticky hands, begging for a snack. Ask any mama who is in the thick of it and she will tell you how easily the mundane cries of her child's neediness begin to pile up. Like the laundry on the couch, a child's appeals for her mother's ears, eyes, feet and hands never seem to end, and as mere mortals, moms eventually fall short of being able to hear and listen to every request.

But not our King. Our God is not limited by flesh. His capacity to listen to our hearts far exceeds that of a mother, father, brother, sister or friend in the flesh who has good intentions. God's ear is unceasingly bent towards His children. He loves the sound of their voices. The ones who know they are loved by Him--who live to love Him and make Him famous on the earth by doing whatever would please His heart--continually have His ear. God, our Father, the good and kind King, loves not only to *listen* to the needs and dreams of His children but also to back His promises by making their requests a reality, always giving something that far exceeds what they asked for. Our King is extravagant with His love and unbothered by the requests of His kids. Our God is the good listener and we are the ones He listens to.

RECOVER: Answer these questions below by journaling your response.

How would I define what it means to be listened to?

_____

_____

_____

Why do I have a hard time believing God hears me?

_____

_____

_____

RE-CREATE:

My hope for this day is _____

Today I will re-create my **mind** by _____

Today I will re-create my **heart** by _____

Today I will re-create my **body** by _____

Today I will bless _____ by _____

REJOICE:

In your journal, write a personal prayer giving thanks to God for what He has done, is doing or will do. Tell Him how wonderful He is! Then ask Him for what you need.

_____

_____

_____

_____

_____

_____

_____

_____

_____

_____

BREATHE: Set a timer for 3-5 minutes. Find a comfortable chair to sit in, close your eyes, and rest your palms open in your lap or in any comfortable position. Inhale and exhale the following prayer:

INHALE – My Father knows all about me
EXHALE – He delights in all He sees

"Come see a man who knew all about the things I did, who knows me inside and out." – John 4:29, MSG

We are made for love and freedom. The common longing of all humanity is to be fully known and fully loved. We are born of the flesh into a fractured world, yet we dream of ways to be celebrated, known and loved. Our hunger for what is true, noble and praiseworthy is evidence that we have eternity placed in our hearts. In our humanness, we make confident promises to love beyond the boundaries our eyes can see. We believe that is what love does and we long for a reciprocated love that will never leave. But humans sometimes fail us. Only God's True Love sees our darkest parts and says, "I'm not leaving. I chose you. Together we will work all things out for good."

God created all of His kids with needs. A child sets out on an exploratory bike ride but always returns home in time for dinner. In the same way, our needs keep us from wandering too far or being gone too long from home. We forfeit our rights as daughters and the peace and power we experience as children of God when we choose to have our legitimate needs met in illegitimate ways. In so doing, we darken our hearts until they no longer can see or sense true love. Jesus, the Prince of Peace, took on flesh to come near to our dark and hungry hearts to show us the way back home to our royal residence where we are safe, fully loved and fully known. In this residence, the Father's tears of joy wipe clean the scrapes we acquired when we got lost and fell down while chasing shadows. Our Father The King is waiting to receive us back into the safety of His love and the power of His wisdom. He longs to tell us everything we never knew about ourselves and everything we need to know to carry our royal identity faithfully. He wants us to steward the riches that we have been given as we carry the family name. The next time we are tempted to wander, we remember: *God loves me and knows me and that is enough for me.*

RECOVER: Answer these questions below by journaling your response.

How do I know God knows me?

What does God see when he looks at me?

RE-CREATE:

My hope for this day is

Today I will re-create my **mind** by

Today I will re-create my **heart** by

Today I will re-create my **body** by

Today I will bless _____ by

REJOICE:

In your journal, write a personal prayer giving thanks to God for what He has done, is doing or will do. Tell Him how wonderful He is! Then ask Him for what you need.

BREATHE: Find a comfortable chair to sit in, close your eyes, and rest your palms open in your lap or in any comfortable position. Inhale and exhale the following prayer:

INHALE – Voice of God speak,
EXHALE – I am listening

"When he has brought out all his own, he goes before them, and the sheep follow him, for they know his voice." – John 10:4, NASB

Sitting in silence is a ninja skill that every daughter of The King must practice often. If you have ever been to an open-air music concert or in any large gathering of people surrounded by lights and loud sounds, you understand why it would be a foolish place to take an important phone call. It is God's voice that separated waters from land, earth from sky, flipped on the sun, and spun the world into motion. He spoke so we could speak. God's voice is still speaking and calling us all out of darkness away from shame, fear, and guilt, and closer to His heart.

As daughters, do we daily sharpen our listening skills to hear the voice of the One who called us His own? Do we use our ears more than our mouth?

Hearing the voice of God is not a trait you are born with like the color of your eyes or the texture of your hair. It's an ability. Just as you have the ability to grow muscle on top of your bones if you intentionally put your body under the stress of added weight, you are capable of growing your ability to hear from God as you draw away from a noisy world and settle your body, heart and mind down, in a quiet place.

RECOVER: Answer these questions below by journaling your response.

How do I practice my skill of hearing from God?

_____
_____
_____

How can I improve my practice?

_____
_____
_____

RE-CREATE:

My hope for this day is _____

Today I will re-create my **mind** by _____

Today I will re-create my **heart** by _____

Today I will re-create my **body** by _____

Today I will bless _____ by _____

REJOICE:

In your journal, write a personal prayer giving thanks to God for what He has done, is doing or will do. Tell Him how wonderful He is! Then ask Him for what you need.'

_____
_____
_____
_____
_____
_____
_____
_____
_____
_____
_____

BREATHE: Set a timer for 3-5 minutes. Find a comfortable chair to sit in, close your eyes, and rest your palms open in your lap or in any comfortable position. Inhale and exhale the following prayer:

INHALE – This world can't take from me
EXHALE – what I have entrusted to God

"But you, O LORD, are a shield about me, my glory, and the lifter of my head." – Psalm 3:3

One thing you must know as a royal daughter of The King is that you are not to put confidence in the flesh or in the things of this physical world. You are a spiritual being, given the gift of a body. The world will bump up against you as you fight the battle to stay noble, loved and true. Some days will leave you battered and bruised. You will see pain, you will feel pain, and any part of your mind still in need of renewal will be tempted to run for cover, fearful of the self-centered lies and worldly rhetoric that cuts you off from the flow of perfect love and truth. The enemy of your King and His Kingdom will come for our sober minds, trying to convince us that our King cannot be trusted or that He isn't good.

What the world can snag, hurt or kill is of no eternal value. As our Prince of Peace has said, "Do not be afraid of those who kill the body but cannot kill the soul" (Matthew 10:28, AMP).

Our lives belong to God. What can the enemy of our souls do to us when we live in the reality that every battle we will face is already won? Our heads stay high when we remember we have transferred possession of our lives to the Father, our King. The very things we hand over to God to take care of cannot be taken. As we rest in His perfect safety, we become trust fund babies – children who inherit His good promises of worth and value that are available to us whenever we need them.

We are saved. All that is valuable is safe. We are the victorious ones!

RECOVER: Answer these questions below by journaling your response.

How safe do I feel with God?

_____

_____

What lie or temptation of the flesh am I believing when I don't feel safe?

_____

_____

_____

RE-CREATE:

My hope for this day is _____

Today I will re-create my **mind** by _____

Today I will re-create my **heart** by _____

Today I will re-create my **body** by _____

Today I will bless _____ by _____

REJOICE:

In your journal, write a personal prayer giving thanks to God for what He has done, is doing or will do. Tell Him how wonderful He is! Then ask Him for what you need.

_____

_____

_____

_____

_____

_____

_____

_____

_____

_____

BREATHE: Set a timer for 3-5 minutes. Find a comfortable chair to sit in, close your eyes, and rest your palms open in your lap or in any comfortable position. Inhale and exhale the following prayer:

INHALE – Love is patient
EXHALE – Love is kind

"Love is patient, love is kind. It does not envy, it does not boast, it is not proud." – 1 Corinthians 13:4, NIV

Just because you are royalty doesn't mean you won't struggle with being human. Your crown does not make you impervious to human suffering and frustration. People won't always do what you want them to do, and circumstances will arise that will make you want to take out your sword and start swinging. You must instead take a breath and line yourself up with love, which is marked by patience and kindness. A woman who knows the crown she wears always lines herself up with love before taking action.

Your Father is not a King who has to prove His love by forcing Himself on people. Unlike the kings of the earth who must strive to prove their worth to man, our Father The King proved man's worth through the love that Christ bled out on the cross. When we were sinners, our King came, fought and won us back! His love is patient, His love is kind. Now we carry on the family tradition of an imperial love that is patient and kind. We have been given the assignment to draw near to those in need and give them the riches of love without imposing heavy taxes on their souls of shame and regret. We are also challenged to offer blessings of love to those who do not deserve it and refuse to receive it, for we were once as cynical in our hearts as they are. Thank God, His love is patient and kind. He shares this love with us as something freely given, so that we are free to give it to others.

RECOVER: Answer these questions below by journaling your response.

In what ways has God's love been unlike the love of the world?

_____

_____

_____

What do I need in order to be more patient and kind with my love?

_____

_____

_____

RE-CREATE:

My hope for this day is _____

Today I will re-create my **mind** by _____

Today I will re-create my **heart** by _____

Today I will re-create my **body** by _____

Today I will bless _____ by _____

REJOICE:

In your journal, write a personal prayer giving thanks to God for what He has done, is doing or will do. Tell Him how wonderful He is! Then ask Him for what you need.

_____

_____

_____

_____

_____

_____

_____

_____

_____

_____

_____

BREATHE: Set a timer for 3-5 minutes. Find a comfortable chair to sit in, close your eyes, and rest your palms open in your lap or in any comfortable position. Inhale and exhale the following prayer:

INHALE – God's got me covered
EXHALE – I am free to cover others

"Do nothing from rivalry or conceit, but in humility count others more significant than yourselves." – Philippians 2:3

A princess who is not obsessed with herself seems almost counterintuitive but those are the ones we love the most. If you think about Disney princesses, we cheer for the ones who don't use their beauty for selfish gain or try to trap and hold hostage the affections of others. Those undesirable character traits are usually found in the antagonist of any great heroine's story. A royal woman who knows who she is does not need to flaunt her beauty or flex her muscles. She knows it's the backing of her King that makes her desirable and strong. Her power comes from within. She knows who she is. She awakens the world around her to what is possible when someone chooses to live within the Kingdom of her King. It's her knowledge of her riches that flow from within that causes her to be a resource for surrounding nations and their people.

Life is not found in what others can do for us but in what we can do for others. A life lived less for self and more for God and others is where abundant life is found. God didn't wait for us to serve Him before He served us, and He didn't wait for us to call Him Father before He called us by name. If you are lacking joy, go find out what your royal Dad is up to. His plans for each day are incredibly good and you are always a part of His plan to love and serve the world. You are a heroine in God's great love story. How will people know of our good and kind King who desires to adopt more sons and daughters unless we go and tell them what we have found? The Kingdom law of love works like this: if you are in need of love, think higher than yourself. Go find someone to love patiently and kindly, and love will come rushing back into your soul, restoring your royal identity.

RECOVER: Answer these questions below by journaling your response.

What are common traps that get me stuck on myself?

_____

_____

_____

What lie do I believe that keeps me focusing on me?

_____

_____

_____

RE-CREATE:

My hope for this day is _____

Today I will re-create my **mind** by _____

_____

Today I will re-create my **heart** by _____

_____

Today I will re-create my **body** by _____

_____

Today I will bless _____ by _____

REJOICE:

In your journal, write a personal prayer giving thanks to God for what He has done, is doing or will do. Tell Him how wonderful He is! Then ask Him for what you need.

_____

_____

_____

_____

_____

_____

_____

_____

_____

_____

BREATHE: Set a timer for 3-5 minutes. Find a comfortable chair to sit in, close your eyes, and rest your palms open in your lap or in any comfortable position. Inhale and exhale the following prayer:

INHALE – I was made to worship God
EXHALE – I love to please His heart

"Sing to the LORD, all the earth; proclaim his salvation day after day. Declare his glory among the nations, his marvelous deeds among all peoples." – 1 Chronicles 16:23-24, NIV

When you hear the word "worship," what comes to mind? Perhaps a stained glass old-world cathedral with the organ music rattling the rafters, with a white robed choir with hymnals open and mouths moving in sync. Or perhaps you picture people of faith, listening to music, singing about God with their arms outstretched. Worship seems like something only the religious do, when in fact, it is something everyone with breath does. Worship occurs anytime and anywhere someone gives their highest devotion of time, talent or treasure to someone or something. Everybody worships and falls prey to worshipping created things rather than Creator God, The One True King.

What does worship have to do with us being royal sons and daughters of God? Everything! By giving over our lives (our time, talent and treasure) to follow Jesus, we each hold a key to our Father's Kingdom, giving us access to unlock the gates of heaven anytime, anywhere. We enter into warfare, fighting our noble fight for what is lovely, true, and right through worship. As God's royal heirs, whenever we open our mouths to speak the language of the Kingdom – words filled with grace and truth – or open our minds to think thoughts of heaven, we are drawing our sword on behalf of The King. When royal children of God open their mouths, minds, bodies and hearts to the things of God, heaven's angel army rises to cover our backs.

For a royal, worship is warfare.

RECOVER: Answer these questions below by journaling your response.

What tries to steal my worship (time, money or energy)?

_____

_____

What can I do to take my worship back and put it where it belongs?

_____

_____

_____

RE-CREATE:

My hope for this day is _____

Today I will re-create my **mind** by _____

Today I will re-create my **heart** by _____

Today I will re-create my **body** by _____

Today I will bless _____ by _____

REJOICE:

In your journal, write a personal prayer giving thanks to God for what He has done, is doing or will do. Tell Him how wonderful He is! Then ask Him for what you need.

_____

_____

_____

_____

_____

_____

_____

_____

_____

_____

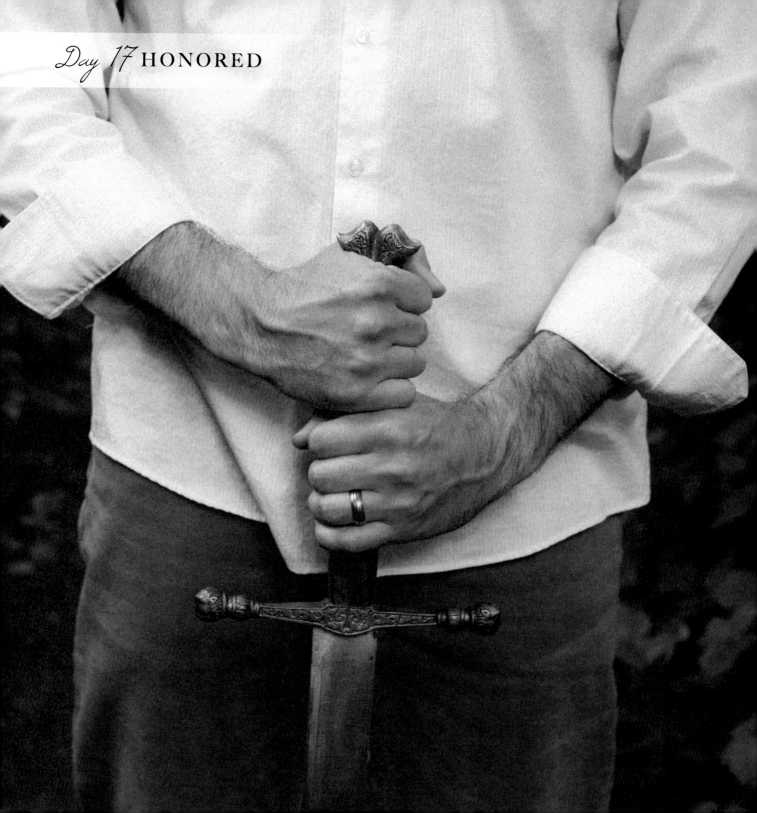

BREATHE: Set a timer for 3-5 minutes. Find a comfortable chair to sit in, close your eyes, and rest your palms open in your lap or in any comfortable position. Inhale and exhale the following prayer:

INHALE – I honor God
EXHALE – God honors me (high-respect, great esteem)

"What is man that you are mindful of him, and the son of man that you care for him? Yet you have made him a little lower than the heavenly beings and crowned him with glory and honor." – Psalm 8:4-5

Wikipedia defines bowing, or stooping, as the act of lowering the torso and head as a social gesture to another person or symbol. It is most prominent in Asian cultures, but it is also typical of nobility and aristocracy in many countries and distinctively in Europe.

Few people on planet earth will ever know what it's like to walk into a room and have heads turn and chatter cease as someone humbly approaches them, bowing to honor their presence. The physical act of bowing our head displays to others and to those honored that in their presence we are more than happy to play second fiddle. The desire to honor, much like worship, is placed inside the heart of every human being. The human heart that is not living in surrendered service to God will honor whomever or whatever they believe will keep them safe.

It's easy for us royal heirs to the throne to accept that bowing our heads to God's heart is part of life. But to think that God honors us? That sounds downright crazy. But it's true. God honors us! Our King thinks highly of his children. He sees who they are as they are becoming who He has fashioned them to be. He knows their flaws and loves them, knowing that they will continue to learn and grow into His royal house rules. Although there are days that His children fall short of the honor that He gives, He never loses sight of who they are becoming. This King refuses to surrender His honor for the people He so dearly loves.

God honors us when we honor Him, and He honors us even when we fall short of giving the honor He deserves. He doesn't turn on and off His esteem for His children like a tyrant who can't be satisfied and needs someone to pay attention to Him. In himself He is satisfied and complete. He doesn't need His children to complete His love, He wants His children to know His love is entirely all they need. When God made us in love, for love, He bowed to us first.

As Jesus was raised up on the cross, God bowed His head. He bowed His head in honor to His Son, Jesus, who became The Door; the entry point to our place of honor at The King's table.

God's people honor God. God honors His people.

RECOVER: Answer these questions below by journaling your response.

What do I think about God honoring me?

_____
_____
_____

What could I do to cultivate more honor in my life?

_____
_____
_____

RE-CREATE:

My hope for this day is _____

Today I will re-create my **mind** by _____

Today I will re-create my **heart** by _____

Today I will re-create my **body** by _____

Today I will bless _____ by _____

REJOICE:

In your journal, write a personal prayer giving thanks to God for what He has done, is doing or will do. Tell Him how wonderful He is! Then ask Him for what you need.

_____
_____
_____
_____
_____

BREATHE: Set a timer for 3-5 minutes. Find a comfortable chair to sit in, close your eyes, and rest your palms open in your lap or in any comfortable position. Inhale and exhale the following prayer:

INHALE – I have been set free
EXHALE – to set free

"Receive the Holy Spirit. If you forgive the sins of any, they are forgiven them; if you withhold forgiveness from any, it is withheld." – John 20:22-23

You are a royal heir to the throne. You did not receive this gift through works but by grace through faith in Christ. Your faith in God's kingdom and the overwhelming power it has to overturn hopeless situations and redeem the hardest of hearts keeps you rooted in truth. You will receive whatever it is you are looking for if it is found behind heaven's gates. You are a lady of liberty, and love and freedom are what you have to offer hurting hearts and hearts that have hurt you.

The Kingdom freedom bell rings wherever the gospel of forgiveness is preached. We are free to be the royal children of God because we have been forgiven – released from the bondage of sin and sentenced to eternal life instead of death. The last thing a royal child would want to do is hold onto offense or refuse to honor another as a dearly loved child of God. Love without freedom is controlling and oppressive, and that is not how a royal child lives as an heir. Those who are royal never forget what The King has done for them. When they were living as paupers on the streets, He came and called them home to live with Him and take the family name. They received their crown by bowing their heads in love and humility to God, and they must do the same for others. Forgiveness releases people to be under the influence of God's Kingdom instead of captive to the pain caused by the sin that fuels the spirit of fear in this world. Exercising the gospel of forgiveness is how the royal family reigns in heaven and grows in favor on the earth.

RECOVER: Answer these questions below by journaling your response.

What is it about freedom that scares me or is hard for me?

_____

_____

_____

What can I do to increase the spirit of freedom in my life?

_____

_____

_____

RE-CREATE:

My hope for this day is _____

Today I will re-create my **mind** by _____

Today I will re-create my **heart** by _____

Today I will re-create my **body** by _____

Today I will bless _____ by _____

REJOICE:

In your journal, write a personal prayer giving thanks to God for what He has done, is doing or will do. Tell Him how wonderful He is! Then ask Him for what you need.

_____

_____

_____

_____

_____

_____

_____

_____

_____

_____

_____

"Strength and dignity are her clothing, and she laughs at the time to come." – Proverbs 31:25

Fighting our holy war of love and freedom will require modesty – a desire to keep some things private. Privacy is a marker of privilege. Just as access to a private country club filled with posh amenities requires membership, so it is for us. Belonging to The King of Glory gives us personal and private access to His heart where not everything we see or hear needs to be shared with others. We must never forget that we are representatives of a beautiful King. We are women who choose to clothe ourselves with strength and dignity. Dressing our hearts with humility gives us the ability to clothe our bodies appropriately.

For a royal, modesty of dress is not being prudish, just as having a humble heart is not a sign of weakness. When we dress our hearts with humility we are best able to serve with The King yet reign like a servant. When we dress our bodies in a way that honors God, who we are as His, and what we have been called to do–we always win the best dressed award.

Before we allow others to view the private and privileged places of our bodies, two things must be required: citizenship to the Kingdom of God (faith in Jesus) and a holy promise (marriage) before their King. Our bodies are a good design given to us by a relational God. Our physicality makes it possible to express what we feel and what we believe and our flesh is the covering for our souls. We care best for our souls when we live as a woman who keeps her clothes on in a world that wants her to take them off. We love others best by keeping our humility of heart on even though others try to set us off.

We royals are on mission in a world that pressures us to show them what they want to see and tell them what they want to hear, when we have been charged to share with them what they truly need - a seat at God's banquet table – a place where proper wear for the body and modesty of the heart is delightfully appealing.

BREATHE: Set a timer for 3-5 minutes. Find a comfortable chair to sit in, close your eyes, and rest your palms open in your lap or in any comfortable position. Inhale and exhale the following prayer:

INHALE – In little or in plenty
EXHALE – it is well with my soul

"I know what it is to be in need, and I know what it is to have plenty. I have learned the secret of being content in any and every situation, whether well fed or hungry, whether living in plenty or in want." – Philippians 4:12, NIV

You need to know that as the daughter of The King, you have an enemy. He's not as obvious as you think. He's not always found picking fights, starting fires and making a mess. He spends most of his time being a busybody. The enemy of your royal life keeps himself busy trying to get the royal family to doubt the sovereignty, goodness and faithfulness of their King. Every day he loads his tranquilizer gun with darts of discontentment hoping to strike the children of God and get them to grumble, curse and complain. When the pain of discomfort arises, do your best to protect your heart from believing the lie that you are not loved, chosen or wanted. That lie belongs in your old life where you once lived as an orphan apart from the high call and kind care of your eternal Father, The King.

All forms of discontentment are a great threat to your inheritance of the throne. From complaining about the shape of your thighs (the seen things) to the pain in your heart (the hidden things) and everything in between, a critical seed takes root and grows rapidly. Before you know it, you will have traded in your royal inheritance for the satisfaction of speaking out your discontent.

The enemy of our royal family does not know what we nobles are thinking, he only knows what we say. He studies what we say then makes a way to get into our hearts through negative thoughts and unbelief.

As God's royal daughter, it is of the utmost importance that you stay alert and pay attention not only to what you say aloud, but to determine where each unsatisfied thought comes from. Is it a lie that stems from your orphan days on the street? If so, hear the invitation from your Father, The King, to climb up on His lap and let Him tell you who you are and remind you of all that you have been given.

Strive to know what it means to be a daughter of God and you won't want to be anyone else but a child of your King.

RECOVER: Answer these questions below by journaling your response.

What things immediately cause me to grumble and complain?

_____
_____
_____

What lie am I believing when I become discontented with my life?

_____
_____
_____

RE-CREATE:

My hope for this day is _____
_____

Today I will re-create my **mind** by _____

Today I will re-create my **heart** by _____

Today I will re-create my **body** by _____

Today I will bless _____ by _____

REJOICE:

In your journal, write a personal prayer giving thanks to God for what He has done, is doing or will do. Tell Him how wonderful He is! Then ask Him for what you need.

_____
_____
_____
_____
_____
_____
_____
_____
_____
_____
_____

BREATHE: Set a timer for 3-5 minutes. Find a comfortable chair to sit in, close your eyes, and rest your palms open in your lap or in any comfortable position. Inhale and exhale the following prayer:

INHALE – Perfect love
EXHALE – Casts out fear

"As you come to him, a living stone rejected by men but in the sight of God chosen and precious." – 1 Peter 2:4

As a royal daughter, get comfortable being uncomfortable. One of the most uncomfortable things a woman can experience is the feeling of being left out. As a royal daughter called for a greater purpose than living for pleasure, there will be times you will need to exercise your right to say "no" and keep your head high when the world says "no" to you. There will be times you won't receive that exclusive invitation to someone else's fancy ball, and times that you will need to say no to someone who is asking you to do something or be someone you are not.

A woman who does not know who she is or who she belongs to will say yes to many things, in hopes of receiving some sense of self-worth and belonging. On the other hand, the royal children of God who are heirs to the throne learn how to say no courageously and how to receive a no graciously in exchange for knowing and belonging to Their King, The One who holds the plans and purposes for their lives.

For a royal daughter who aims to grow in God's perfect love, there is no fear. FOMO is something we know the world battles with, but not something we identify with. When we are left out, it is for the purpose of keeping our crown on and remaining as an heir to the throne. When our answer is no, we will not fear rejection. When the world says "no" to us, we will not fear missing out. We do not fear; we love, and our love is being perfected by the Perfect King.

All of God's Kingdom stands with a daughter's "yes" and all of His angel army backs up her "no."

We are FANS of missing out.

RECOVER: Answer these questions below by journaling your response.

How has fear thwarted my courage to say no and limited my kindness when told "no"?

_____

_____

What truths do I need to understand about saying "no" and about my fear of missing out?

_____

_____

RE-CREATE:

My hope for this day is _____

Today I will re-create my **mind** by _____

Today I will re-create my **heart** by _____

Today I will re-create my **body** by _____

Today I will bless _____ by _____

REJOICE:

In your journal, write a personal prayer giving thanks to God for what He has done, is doing or will do. Tell Him how wonderful He is! Then ask Him for what you need.

_____

_____

_____

_____

_____

_____

_____

_____

BREATHE: Set a timer for 3-5 minutes. Find a comfortable chair to sit in, close your eyes, and rest your palms open in your lap or in any comfortable position. Inhale and exhale the following prayer:

INHALE – Here I am Lord
EXHALE – Today I start again

"Repent, therefore, and turn back, that your sins may be blotted out, that times of refreshing may come." – Acts 3:19

Even though you are a princess, you won't *do* royalty perfectly. You still have your flesh to contend with. Taking ownership of your throne will be an ongoing process of dying to yourself for the sake of another, because that's what the high call of love compels us to do. Do not expect perfection even though you wear a crown. Some days the noise of this world – the voices of fear, shame, and guilt – will interfere with your ability to hear the airwaves of heaven that direct your steps for the cause of the Kingdom.

In the moments when you struggle to hear clearly where to go and what to do next, that struggle is your cue to make the time to be still. Lean in to hear the voice of your heart. If your heart is centered on the peace of Christ, then the Holy Spirit frees you from accusations of fear, shame and guilt, and you can begin to course-correct. You can start to see clearly where you went off course and abandoned the cause of the Kingdom. You can get back in line with your Kingdom identity and purpose; back on the path that leads to life and away from the road that leads to destruction. This is all about repentance – being people who are quick to turn around and go back to our identity, rooted in being royal daughters of God, The King.

Repentance always brings refreshment – fresh ways of seeing, hearing, thinking, feeling and doing. Like a cold drink of water for a soul in a sun-scorched land, repentance is the way back to the road that leads us home to our castle and our King.

RECOVER: Answer these questions below by journaling your response.

What often pulls me off course?

_____
_____
_____

What keeps me from wanting to turn around?

_____
_____
_____

What can I do more quickly and confidently to correct my course?

_____
_____
_____

RE-CREATE:

My hope for this day is _____
_____

Today I will re-create my **mind** by _____
_____

Today I will re-create my **heart** by _____
_____

Today I will re-create my **body** by _____
_____

Today I will bless _____ by _____
_____

REJOICE:

In your journal, write a personal prayer giving thanks to God for what He has done, is doing or will do. Tell Him how wonderful He is! Then ask Him for what you need.

_____
_____
_____
_____
_____
_____
_____
_____

BREATHE: Set a timer for 3-5 minutes. Find a comfortable chair to sit in, close your eyes, and rest your palms open in your lap or in any comfortable position. Inhale and exhale the following prayer:

INHALE – What I look for
EXHALE – I will find

"Now faith is confidence in what we hope for and assurance about what we do not see." – Hebrews 11:1, NIV

Health is never determined by the number on a scale, the size of your wardrobe, or how many muscles you can see in the mirror. Health begins in the heart, grows from the heart, and is measured by the weight of your heart. Your heart was designed to carry around the weight of The King's glory, giving it away freely as others have need. It's best that we get comfortable with sweat, because each of us, as a royal emissary, is in an ongoing boot camp. We are entering into places where the weight of the world stretches and grows our hearts so that hope can remain, and faith can increase. Health starts in the heart: the place where your hope can either be lost or found.

In the Kingdom, hope is not a wishful request. It is not like closing our eyes and blowing out a candle on our birthday cake. In the Kingdom, hope is a certainty, a law. As much as gravity is the assurance that what goes up will come down, hope is a certainty that whatever you are looking for, you will find. Though you might not see what you have hoped for come to pass when you ask, you can be rest assured that a regal hope-filled request will be heaven's delight to answer. When you ask for things that matter to your heart and are in line with The King's best, you can know it will come to pass.

Hope is our lifeline that keeps us connected to the culture of honor we represent and the homeland that we came from.

RECOVER: Answer these questions below by journaling your response.

How do I know when I am living with a hope-filled heart?

_____
_____
_____

What can I do to grow healthy in hope?

_____
_____
_____

RE-CREATE:

My hope for this day is _____

Today I will re-create my **mind** by _____

Today I will re-create my **heart** by _____

Today I will re-create my **body** by _____

Today I will bless _____ by _____

REJOICE:

In your journal, write a personal prayer giving thanks to God for what He has done, is doing or will do. Tell Him how wonderful He is! Then ask Him for what you need.

_____
_____
_____
_____
_____
_____
_____
_____
_____
_____
_____
_____
_____

BREATHE: Set a timer for 3-5 minutes. Find a comfortable chair to sit in, close your eyes, and rest your palms open in your lap or in any comfortable position. Inhale and exhale the following prayer:

INHALE – Every challenge I face
EXHALE – Is already under God's feet

"The Lord said to my Lord, 'Sit at my right hand, until I make your enemies your footstool.'" – Acts 2:34-35

Every royal throne comes with a small red velvet tufted footstool with gold fringe. No throne is complete without one of these rest stops for a royal's feet. Not only is elevating our feet comfortable, but placing our feet on something signifies a finished work, like putting our feet up on the couch at the end of a workday. Not only is it a posture of rest, but the body language of placing your royal feet on your tufted footstool also expresses your authority. This simple action communicates to your fellow countrymen and women that you have no intention of making much of your enemies by allowing them to distress you. As The King's Queen, you are quite aware that all your enemies are already UNDER your feet.

There's a reason the people of Britain are known for the saying "Keep calm and carry on." For a Kingdom woman, staying calm and carrying on does not mean she disengages from the problem at hand by withdrawing to a quiet corner of the palace and hiding out until the trouble passes. Nor does it mean she withdraws to the entertainment room to numb out with excess pleasure. No, a good Queen stays present to the pain of the people around her while seeking the presence of her King, the Prince of Peace. He set her throne next to His for this very purpose; that she might always be at His right hand. He gave her the power of peace and the authority to rest. There's something so powerfully dignified about a woman who does not fall prey to the landmines of the enemy but keeps her confidence secure in the Lord. May we all grow to be that kind of Kingdom woman!

RECOVER: Answer these questions below by journaling your response.

What authority do I know I have in life?

_____
_____
_____

How does my reaction to fear, stress or worry affect myself and others around me?

_____
_____
_____

RE-CREATE:

My hope for this day is _____

Today I will re-create my **mind** by _____

Today I will re-create my **heart** by _____

Today I will re-create my **body** by _____

Today I will bless _____ by _____

REJOICE:

In your journal, write a personal prayer giving thanks to God for what He has done, is doing or will do. Tell Him how wonderful He is! Then ask Him for what you need.

_____
_____
_____
_____
_____
_____
_____
_____
_____
_____
_____
_____
_____

BREATHE: Set a timer for 3-5 minutes. Find a comfortable chair to sit in, close your eyes, and rest your palms open in your lap or in any comfortable position. Inhale and exhale the following prayer:

INHALE – I carry the sword of God's Word
EXHALE – and the shield of faith

"In all circumstances take up the shield of faith, with which you can extinguish all the flaming darts of the evil one....and the sword of the Spirit, which is the word of God..." – Ephesians 6:16,17

You are a princess and you are armed. You are dangerous to the forces of darkness that try to steal your identity and your place as a royal at the family table. The world has never seen a princess like you. You're not as interested in the clothing you wear as you are in using the weapons you carry. An armed woman who does not know who she is will use weapons to evoke fear in the heart of her captives, but we, as royal daughters of The King, have no interest in taking prisoners. We use our weapons to aid us in our call to set captives free even as we use them to free ourselves from things that bind us.

You are a two-fisted royal, carrying a shield in one hand and a sword in the other. Can you see it? Close your eyes now and see yourself standing on the victor's hill with trained weapons of warfare in your hands; a shield engraved with the family crest covering your chest and a glistening sword raised high. It's this family shield of faith that protected you when your orphaned heart showed up and tempted you to surrender to the barking hounds of hell nipping at your feet. Your faith – your certainty that The King stands behind your heart even if you are not yet standing in victory – is your shield. It's your faith that protects you from surrendering your identity as a daughter of The King and from disconnecting from the power and authority you have in His name. It's the sword of the Spirit, which is the spoken Word of God, stored up in your heart that keeps you free. That Word will rise up from within you when hell tries to come against you. Keep your sword sharp by grinding it daily against what God has said; read the words that can be found in The Bible, His royal book. Each day, remember to sharpen your sword and raise your shield. Always stand ready for the battle trumpet to blow.

God, our good and gracious King, will be faithful to back every word He has spoken. Everything written down in His Word and every word He is speaking to your heart; He will be faithful to fulfill.

You are an armed princess, a queen, a woman dressed for the battle of bringing heaven down to earth.

RECOVER: Answer these questions below by journaling your response.

What are my first go-to weapons when faced with opposition?

_____

_____

What is God trying to teach me about how to use my shield and my sword?

_____

_____

RE-CREATE:

My hope for this day is _____

Today I will re-create my **mind** by _____

Today I will re-create my **heart** by _____

Today I will re-create my **body** by _____

Today I will bless _____ by _____

REJOICE:

In your journal, write a personal prayer giving thanks to God for what He has done, is doing or will do. Tell Him how wonderful He is! Then ask Him for what you need.

_____

_____

_____

_____

_____

_____

BREATHE: Set a timer for 3-5 minutes. Find a comfortable chair to sit in, close your eyes, and rest your palms open in your lap or in any comfortable position. Inhale and exhale the following prayer:

INHALE – I will feel my pain
EXHALE – and not do my pain

"We rejoice in our sufferings, knowing that suffering produces endurance, and endurance produces character, and character produces hope, and hope does not put us to shame, because God's love has been poured into our hearts through the Holy Spirit who has been given to us." – Romans 5:3-5

Having all the rights and privileges as a triumphant child in God's monarchy while still being a militant foot-soldier on earth will bring your soul into great conflict from time to time. Your identity as a daughter of The King does not release you from feeling the pain of this world. Being in this world but not of it does not prevent you from experiencing the suffering that comes with the effects of sin and darkness. This is the darkness that infects the hearts of those who have yet to know they are loved by our extravagant King.

The best representatives of God's Kingdom are not afraid to feel pain. It's important that you learn how to feel pain without feeding it or inflicting pain on others. When the sting of this world hits you, do not be quick to run to some form of pain relief. Don't lash out like a madwoman or sneak out the back door, climbing into your luxury car as the motorcade whisks you away. Learning how to lean into pain is what matures a child princess into a warrior queen. All the hurt you feel is there to teach you something that will help you become who God intends you to be. When someone refuses to treat you as the royalty you are, says unkind things about you, or challenges your value and worth, get violent by taking a moment to be still, grow strong, and breathe. Then take the hurt by the hand to the throne room, where you get to exchange it for the hope that never puts you or another to shame.

Hope extinguishes pain in all the right ways.

RECOVER: Answer these questions below by journaling your response.

What do I think about suffering?

_____
_____
_____

What is God asking me to do with the pain that I feel?

_____
_____
_____

RE-CREATE:

My hope for this day is _____

Today I will re-create my **mind** by _____

Today I will re-create my **heart** by _____

Today I will re-create my **body** by _____

Today I will bless _____ by _____

REJOICE:

In your journal, write a personal prayer giving thanks to God for what He has done, is doing or will do. Tell Him how wonderful He is! Then ask Him for what you need.

_____
_____
_____
_____
_____
_____
_____
_____
_____
_____
_____
_____

BREATHE: Set a timer for 3-5 minutes. Find a comfortable chair to sit in, close your eyes, and rest your palms open in your lap or in any comfortable position. Inhale and exhale the following prayer:

INHALE – The King gives me His joy
EXHALE – I will enjoy my life

"And the streets of the city shall be full of boys and girls playing in its streets." – Zechariah 8:5

The question of whether or not you are an heir to the throne is not up for debate. God says you are His (Matthew 3:17) and all that is His is yours (Romans 8:17). You are a part of God's monarchy now, a royal priesthood, a people for His own possession (1 Peter 2:9). The question of whether or not you enjoy your lot in life as a royal is an important concept to consider daily. It leaves a bitter taste in our mouths when we see spoiled children who lose sight of how blessed they really are. When we focus too much on the pain and struggle in our lives, we are on the cusp of forgetting who we are. When we forget who we are, we will abandon the wonder, awe, and fun of living like loved children. Mature daughters of The King grow in power and wisdom and bless the world around them when they keep the spirit of play, wonder, and adventure alive.

You're never too old, too rich, or in too hard a situation to run, laugh and play.

Daughter of The King, make it your assignment to enjoy your life. Schedule fun it into your day by setting aside times to rest, relax and play. Whether you choose to get muddy and climb a mountain or get pretty and put on a fancy dress, make sure you do whatever is needed to keep your Kingdom joy alive. If it has been awhile since you have belly-laughed, it might be time to ask yourself "What do I enjoy doing?" or "What was I doing the last time I had joy and felt free?" Then go do it again! Joy is the remedy for an entitled, bitter and spoiled royal heart, and it's the joy of your King that gives you strength. The enemy of your Father's Kingdom flees at the sound of laughter. Let the Kingdom streets ring with the sounds of joy!

RECOVER: Answer these questions below by journaling your response.

What do I enjoy doing?

_____

_____

What was I doing the last time I belly laughed?

_____

_____

What do I need to do to increase joy in my life?

_____

_____

RE-CREATE:

My hope for this day is _____

Today I will re-create my **mind** by _____

Today I will re-create my **heart** by _____

Today I will re-create my **body** by _____

Today I will bless _____ by _____

REJOICE:

In your journal, write a personal prayer giving thanks to God for what He has done, is doing or will do. Tell Him how wonderful He is! Then ask Him for what you need.

_____

_____

_____

_____

_____

_____

_____

_____

BREATHE: Set a timer for 3-5 minutes. Find a comfortable chair to sit in, close your eyes, and rest your palms open in your lap or in any comfortable position. Inhale and exhale the following prayer:

INHALE – I am filled
EXHALE – with righteousness, peace and joy

"For the kingdom of God is not a matter of eating and drinking, but of righteousness, peace and joy in the Holy Spirit." – Romans 14:17, NIV

Getting a yearly physical check-up is a good idea for those called to do important things. The people they serve can rest easy knowing their loved and needed leader is in good health, ready for the job at hand. When visiting a doctor, you can expect that your vital signs will be checked, including pulse rate and body temperature. These readings tell us if we are healthy on the inside, regardless of how the outside appears. In addition to the physical report, the inner person – the site of our motives and decisions – is of great importance to every man and woman.

You are a royal, not a superhero. This means you will face struggles like other men and women face. There will be days you will feel under the weather. There will be days when battles against the Kingdom – including greed, selfishness, fear, lust and hate of brother against brother or sister against sister – appear bigger than the providence of the Sovereign One you serve.

When you feel under the weather or unable to fulfill your engagements for the day, be sure to get to the Royal Physician's office as soon as possible. If the sickness is so intense that you can't get out of bed, you can call Him, and He will come to you. He loves a good house call. Once in His care, you can expect Him to check the vitals of your inner-self: your righteousness, peace, and joy. He checks our righteousness by asking us if we remember who The King says we are and reminding us of the price He paid in Christ to call us His own. He checks our peace by asking us to sit still and take deep breaths, remembering the love of our King who called us into His family care. Finally, He checks our joy by seeing if He can make us laugh. After all, the battles we will face have already been won at the cross. The tactics of our enemy to destroy us are laughable at best. And laughter is our Physician's favorite kind of medicine.

RECOVER: Answer these questions below by journaling your response.

How do I usually measure how well I am doing?

_____
_____
_____

How are my vitals of righteousness, peace, and joy doing right now?

_____
_____
_____

RE-CREATE:

My hope for this day is _____

Today I will re-create my **mind** by _____

Today I will re-create my **heart** by _____

Today I will re-create my **body** by _____

Today I will bless _____ by _____

REJOICE:

In your journal, write a personal prayer giving thanks to God for what He has done, is doing or will do. Tell Him how wonderful He is! Then ask Him for what you need.

_____
_____
_____
_____
_____
_____
_____
_____
_____
_____
_____
_____
_____
_____
_____

BREATHE: Set a timer for 3-5 minutes. Find a comfortable chair to sit in, close your eyes, and rest your palms open in your lap or in any comfortable position. Inhale and exhale the following prayer:

INHALE – I have the strength
EXHALE – to hold peace

"Your beauty should not come from outward adornment, such as elaborate hairstyles and the wearing of gold jewelry or fine clothes. Rather, it should be that of your inner self, the unfading beauty of a gentle and quiet spirit, which is of great worth in God's sight."
– 1 Peter 3:3-4, NIV

Don't worry, royal daughter. Your King is not saying you can't have fun getting dressed up in pretty clothes and fancy shoes while throwing your hair up in a messy bun. All of those things are good and fun. Even our queen mother, Esther, was treated to a time of beauty at the King's parlor. This verse is a reminder that your King is enthralled with your beauty. It's a beauty that begins inside, in a quiet and gentle space, revealing itself on the outside in a way that is true to who you are and honors The One whom you love and serve.

Gentle is not a popular word in a world that believes that only the strongest survive. "Go big or go home" comes across as "Get big or get chewed up!" We royal women of battle often recoil at the word gentle, but that is because we have missed the King's meaning of the word. The Greek word for gentle that Paul uses to instruct means "mildness of disposition." Gentleness is a quality of those who wholly rely on God's strength rather than their own in order to defend injustice. It takes great inner strength to stand down so that the strength of God can stand up.

Next, Paul uses the word quiet. We modern royals rage against the thought of someone telling us to be quiet. It sounds downright rude! But in the Greek, the word quiet does not mean to shut up, but to "keep one's seat." In other words, our King has assigned each of us a royal position of importance and prominence in the Kingdom. We each have a throne and through the Word, learn more of what it means to rule and reign in the Kingdom. We are called to use our voices, but never at the cost of losing our seat.

Some of our sisters will bypass the beauty parlor and strap on boots for a dusty hike in the hills. But no matter what we do with our outer life, whether we dress it up or dress it down, we are women of an inner glorious strength, women who trust God and so get more and more

strength from Him. There's no need for us to shout louder or run faster after an enemy who wants to bait us into "getting big" and giving up our seat.

Stay strong in His strength, royal daughter. Stay strong and seated on your throne. This is of great worth in your King's sight.

RECOVER: Answer these questions below by journaling your response.

Before reading today's devotional, how did you feel about this verse?

_____

_____

_____

After reading today's devotional what traps does God want you to avoid about being of a gentle and quiet spirit?

_____

_____

_____

RE-CREATE:

My hope for this day is _____

Today I will re-create my **mind** by _____

Today I will re-create my **heart** by _____

Today I will re-create my **body** by _____

Today I will bless _____ by _____

REJOICE:

In your journal, write a personal prayer giving thanks to God for what He has done, is doing or will do. Tell Him how wonderful He is! Then ask Him for what you need.

_____

_____

_____

_____

BREATHE: Set a timer for 3-5 minutes. Find a comfortable chair to sit in, close your eyes, and rest your palms open in your lap or in any comfortable position. Inhale and exhale the following prayer:

INHALE – I know The King and The King knows me
EXHALE – I am free

"If you abide in my word, you are truly my disciples, and you will know the truth, and the truth will set you free." – John 8:31-32

There's an old American patriotic song written by Frank Loesser titled "Praise The Lord and Pass The Ammunition." I think that those words are fitting as we head into this last day of training as royal heirs, people of God's promise. Those two statements joined together by the word "and" give good guidance to how we proceed as viceroys of a Godly Kingdom here on earth.

If you want to inherit fully what God has promised you, then at all times, and at all costs, keep praising the Lord. Those who stay close to Him and remain with Him in the family home enjoy His company. Their hearts will constantly speak the praises of their good, kind, and gracious King. People who abide in Christ find endless reasons to get out of bed and hit the streets with a royal purpose for each day.

Keep reminding yourself that God first brought you in from the streets and called you His own. He gave you your own room in the royal palace and dressed you with the finest robe, sandals, and ring. He knew what He was looking for when He came looking for you, and you responded to the call of His voice. Praise the Lord! You no longer live for yourself but for this King!

All around you are reasons to stir up your excitement for The King and His Kingdom. What you look for, you will find. Keep reading the words He has spoken in the Bible and keep listening for the voice of the Living Word, King Jesus, who through the power of God's Holy Spirit in you, is still speaking to you today. Praise the Lord! Let everything with breath praise the Lord, always in all ways! Praise reminds you of the love of your good King and tunes your heart to your identity and your inheritance.

Finally, don't forget to pass the ammunition. You are in a spiritual war. The world is going to fight against the knowledge of this great King of ours. We can never forget that we do not fight against flesh and blood, but spiritual forces of evil (Ephesians 6:12). We are fighting a spiritual battle for the many who have not accepted the truth of Christ The King. The ammunition we need to carry for freedom's sake are these:

Stay Humble – remain teachable by surrendering to the desires of the Holy Spirit and be forgiving of others who wrong you. Jesus even forgave those who drove the nails into his flesh.

God's Word – read it first and read it often. It will always lift your heart in praise and renew your mind in the knowledge of The King.

Prayer – this can be as simple as the breathing prayers we have been doing each day. Keep your conversation alive all day with your King! He loves the sound of your voice.

Other Royals – find a royal family table on earth (a church community) and gather there often. Let the trusted elders of the royal family speak into your life and provide the love and truth you need on the days you feel weak.

Have fun! – if your joy gets stolen, it's probably because you've made abiding in God complicated. He has called you into His family so that you can know His love and return His love with joy. Put all the royal duties aside and seek to just be His kid. He is most interested in having you walk with Him first, and then work with Him from the secure place of knowing how loved you are. Be of glad heart! Your King is the King of Kings!

Now, all you royal daughters, praise the Lord and pass the ammunition!

RECOVER: Answer these questions below by journaling your response.

What can you praise God for?

_____
_____
_____

Which ammunition do you need more of?

_____
_____
_____

RE-CREATE:

My hope for this day is _____

Today I will re-create my **mind** by _____

Today I will re-create my **heart** by _____

Today I will re-create my **body** by _____

Today I will bless _____ by _____

REJOICE:

In your journal, write a personal prayer giving thanks to God for what He has done, is doing or will do. Tell Him how wonderful He is! Then ask Him for what you need.

_____
_____
_____
_____
_____
_____
_____
_____
_____
_____
_____

You did it! You have completed *Heir to the Crown: A Mind-Body Devotional for the Daughters of God*. My hope and prayer is that you have recovered your identity as a daughter of the King, are being re-created from the inside out, take time rejoice in worship, and respond by sharing what you have learned by blessing others.

I would be honored for you to leave an honest review of this devotional so we can keep improving and advancing His Kingdom.

With gratitude,

Alisa Keeton

ABOUT THE AUTHOR

Alisa is a wholehearted pursuer of God's love. After more than twenty-give years as a fitness professional, Alisa felt God leading her to bring fresh meaning to the world of health and fitness. At first she resisted, but eventually she got on her knees, rolled up her sleeves, and followed His call. In 2011, she launched Revelation Wellness. This nonprofit ministry uses fitness as a tool to spread the gospel message, inviting participants to become whole and live well. The Revelation Wellness instructor training program equips and sends out "fitness missionaries" throughout the United States and around the world, while RevWell TV brings faith-based online workouts and resources to anyone with Internet access.

Alisa lives in Phoenix with her husband, Simon, and their two children, Jack and Sophia. As a family, they are on mission to change the world with the kind and courageous love of God.

You can connect with Alisa at AlisaKeeton.com and @alisakeeton on Instagram, Facebook, or Twitter.

Continue the health and wholeness journey with Alisa's book, *"The Wellness Revelation: Lose What Weighs You Down So You Can Love God, Yourself, and Others"* available wherever books are sold.

OTHER OFFERINGS OF REVELATION WELLNESS

REVELATION WELLNESS INSTRUCTOR TRAINING

Our nine-week instructor-training course thoroughly equips leaders of all ages, experience levels, and styles to use fitness as a tool to spread the Good News of the gospel message.

www.revelationwellness.org/rwit

LIVE REVELATION FITNESS CLASSES AND WELLNESS REVELATION FACILITATORS

Find a Revelation Fitness class or Wellness Revelation facilitator near you.

www.revelationwellness.org/find-classes/

REVWELL TV

Can't get to a live Revelation Fitness class? Become a monthly partner with Revelation Wellness! Our gift of thanks to you is online access to more than one hundred faith-filled workouts, workshops, wellness resources, and Bible studies.

www.revelationwellness.org/revwell-tv

FREE 7 DAY DETOX

Join Alisa Keeton for 7 days of teaching videos, assignments, and training sessions to equip you with everything you need for a fresh start to a healthy and whole life.

www.revelationwellness.org/challenges/free-7daydetox/

PODCAST

Push play for regular life-giving interviews, messages, and REVING the Word for your next walk, run, hike, or bike to hear God's Word through workout and worship.

www.revelationwellness.org/workout/podcast-2/

REVELATION WELLNESS EVENTS

RIM TO HIM

Rim to Him is a one-of-a-kind, coed adventure/fund-raiser that culminates in a one-day hike of the Grand Canyon. Our five-month training program is designed to prepare you in heart, mind, soul, and strength to cross one of the wonders of the world! "With God all things are possible" (Matthew 19:26, NIV).

www.revelationwellness.org/events/r2h

REV ON THE ROAD

Rev on the Road is a two-day outreach and wellness event designed to restore people's hope, faith, and love as image bearers of a good and whole God. Invite Revelation Wellness to come to your city and start a Holy Spirit fire of freedom!

www.revelationwellness.org/events/rotr/

MEET UP

A Revelation Wellness Meet Up is an in-person workshop/training. Certified instructors around the world will host local gatherings in their communities. The event includes movement, Biblical teaching, worship, and face-to-face connection with others. Find your people. Love your people.

www.revelationwellness.org/events/meet-up/

More Thoughts

Made in the USA
San Bernardino, CA
06 September 2018